EMMANUEL JOSEPH

Horizons Unbound, How Crypto is Redrawing the Map of Global Trade

Copyright © 2025 by Emmanuel Joseph

All rights reserved. No part of this publication may be reproduced, stored or transmitted in any form or by any means, electronic, mechanical, photocopying, recording, scanning, or otherwise without written permission from the publisher. It is illegal to copy this book, post it to a website, or distribute it by any other means without permission.

First edition

*This book was professionally typeset on Reedsy.
Find out more at reedsy.com*

Contents

1	Chapter 1: The Dawn of a New Era	1
2	Chapter 2: The Technology Behind the Revolution	3
3	Chapter 3: The Fall of Intermediaries	5
4	Chapter 4: The Rise of Decentralized Finance (DeFi)	7
5	Chapter 5: The Geopolitical Implications of Crypto	9
6	Chapter 6: The Role of Stablecoins in Global Trade	11
7	Chapter 7: The Impact of Crypto on Supply Chains	13
8	Chapter 8: The Future of Trade Finance	15
9	Chapter 9: The Role of Central Bank Digital Currencies...	17
10	Chapter 10: The Environmental Impact of Crypto	19
11	Chapter 11: The Role of Regulation in Shaping the Future of...	21
12	Chapter 12: The Future of Global Trade in a Crypto-Driven...	23
13	Epilogue: The Journey Ahead	25

1

Chapter 1: The Dawn of a New Era

The world of global trade has always been shaped by the tools and systems that facilitate it. From the barter system to the gold standard, and from fiat currencies to digital payment platforms, each evolution has redefined how nations and individuals exchange value. Cryptocurrency, however, is not just another step in this progression—it is a seismic shift. Born out of the 2008 financial crisis, Bitcoin introduced the concept of decentralized finance, challenging the very foundations of traditional banking and trade. For the first time in history, value could be transferred across borders without intermediaries, without borders, and without the constraints of centralized control. This chapter explores the origins of cryptocurrency and its potential to disrupt the global trade landscape.

As the first Bitcoin transaction took place in 2009, few could have predicted the ripple effects it would create. Satoshi Nakamoto's vision of a peer-to-peer electronic cash system was not just a technological innovation; it was a philosophical statement. It questioned the necessity of trust in centralized institutions and proposed a system where trust was embedded in code. This idea resonated with a world increasingly skeptical of traditional financial systems. By 2013, Bitcoin had gained traction not just as a speculative asset but as a medium of exchange. Early adopters began using it to purchase goods and services, and businesses started accepting it as payment. The seeds of a new global trade system had been sown.

The implications for global trade were profound. Traditional trade relies heavily on banks, payment processors, and regulatory frameworks that often slow down transactions and increase costs. Cryptocurrencies, by contrast, operate on decentralized networks that are borderless and operate 24/7. This chapter delves into the early experiments with crypto in trade, from small-scale peer-to-peer transactions to the first instances of cross-border trade using Bitcoin. It also examines the challenges faced by these early adopters, including volatility, regulatory uncertainty, and technological limitations.

Despite these challenges, the potential of cryptocurrency to revolutionize global trade became increasingly apparent. By eliminating intermediaries, crypto promised to reduce transaction costs, increase speed, and provide greater financial inclusion. For developing nations, in particular, this was a game-changer. Remittances, which often incur high fees, could now be sent and received at a fraction of the cost. Small businesses could access global markets without the need for expensive banking infrastructure. The dawn of a new era in global trade had arrived, and it was powered by cryptocurrency.

This chapter concludes by setting the stage for the rest of the book. It introduces the key themes that will be explored: the technological underpinnings of cryptocurrency, its impact on traditional financial systems, the rise of decentralized finance (DeFi), and the geopolitical implications of a crypto-driven global trade system. The journey ahead is one of discovery, challenge, and opportunity, as we explore how crypto is redrawing the map of global trade.

2

Chapter 2: The Technology Behind the Revolution

At the heart of the cryptocurrency revolution lies blockchain technology, a decentralized ledger that records transactions across a network of computers. This chapter delves into the technical foundations of blockchain, explaining how it works and why it is so transformative. Unlike traditional databases, which are controlled by a single entity, a blockchain is maintained by a distributed network of nodes. Each transaction is verified by consensus, ensuring transparency and security. This decentralized nature eliminates the need for intermediaries, making it ideal for global trade.

The concept of smart contracts, introduced by Ethereum in 2015, further expanded the possibilities of blockchain technology. Smart contracts are self-executing agreements with the terms of the contract directly written into code. They automatically execute when predefined conditions are met, eliminating the need for intermediaries and reducing the risk of fraud. This innovation opened the door to a wide range of applications in global trade, from supply chain management to trade finance. For example, a smart contract could automatically release payment to a supplier once goods are delivered and verified, streamlining the entire process.

However, the technology is not without its challenges. Scalability remains a significant issue, as blockchain networks struggle to handle large volumes of transactions quickly and efficiently. Energy consumption is another concern, particularly for proof-of-work blockchains like Bitcoin. This chapter explores the ongoing efforts to address these challenges, from the development of more efficient consensus mechanisms to the rise of layer-2 solutions like the Lightning Network. It also examines the role of interoperability in creating a seamless global trade ecosystem, where different blockchains can communicate and transact with one another.

The chapter also highlights the role of cryptography in securing blockchain networks. Cryptography ensures that transactions are secure, private, and tamper-proof. It is the backbone of trust in the system, enabling users to transact with confidence even in the absence of a central authority. This section explains the basics of cryptographic techniques like hashing, digital signatures, and public-private key pairs, providing readers with a deeper understanding of how blockchain technology works.

In conclusion, this chapter emphasizes the transformative potential of blockchain technology in global trade. By providing a secure, transparent, and efficient way to record and verify transactions, blockchain is laying the foundation for a new era of trade. The technology is still evolving, but its impact is already being felt across industries. As we move forward, the continued development and adoption of blockchain technology will play a crucial role in redrawing the map of global trade.

3

Chapter 3: The Fall of Intermediaries

One of the most significant impacts of cryptocurrency on global trade is the elimination of intermediaries. Traditional trade relies on a complex web of banks, payment processors, and regulatory bodies, each adding layers of cost and complexity. This chapter explores how cryptocurrency is disrupting this model, enabling direct peer-to-peer transactions that are faster, cheaper, and more efficient. By cutting out the middlemen, crypto is democratizing access to global markets and empowering individuals and businesses alike.

The role of banks in global trade has long been a contentious issue. While they provide essential services like financing and risk management, they also charge hefty fees and often slow down the process. Cryptocurrencies offer an alternative by enabling direct transactions between parties. For example, a manufacturer in China can now receive payment directly from a buyer in the United States without going through a bank. This not only reduces costs but also speeds up the process, as transactions can be completed in minutes rather than days.

Payment processors like PayPal and Western Union have also been disrupted by the rise of cryptocurrency. These companies charge high fees for cross-border transactions, particularly for remittances. Cryptocurrencies, by contrast, allow for near-instant transfers at a fraction of the cost. This has been a game-changer for migrant workers sending money home to their families. In countries with weak banking infrastructure, crypto has provided a lifeline, enabling financial inclusion and economic empowerment.

However, the fall of intermediaries is not without its challenges. Regulatory bodies play a crucial role in ensuring the integrity of the financial system, and their absence in the crypto space has led to concerns about fraud, money laundering, and tax evasion. This chapter examines the regulatory landscape for cryptocurrency, exploring the efforts of governments and international organizations to create a framework that balances innovation with security. It also looks at the role of decentralized autonomous organizations (DAOs) in filling the gap left by traditional intermediaries.

In conclusion, this chapter highlights the profound impact of cryptocurrency on the role of intermediaries in global trade. By enabling direct peer-to-peer transactions, crypto is reducing costs, increasing efficiency, and democratizing access to global markets. However, the transition is not without its challenges, and the role of regulation will be crucial in shaping the future of this new trade ecosystem. As we move forward, the fall of intermediaries will continue to be a defining feature of the crypto-driven global trade system.

4

Chapter 4: The Rise of Decentralized Finance (DeFi)

Decentralized finance, or DeFi, is one of the most exciting developments in the cryptocurrency space. This chapter explores how DeFi is transforming the financial landscape, offering a wide range of services—from lending and borrowing to trading and insurance—without the need for traditional financial institutions. Built on blockchain technology, DeFi platforms operate on smart contracts, enabling transparent, secure, and efficient financial transactions. This section delves into the key components of DeFi and its implications for global trade.

One of the most significant advantages of DeFi is its accessibility. Traditional financial systems often exclude individuals and businesses that lack access to banking infrastructure. DeFi, by contrast, is open to anyone with an internet connection. This has the potential to revolutionize global trade by providing financial services to underserved populations. For example, a small farmer in Africa can now access a global lending platform to secure a loan for seeds and equipment, bypassing the need for a local bank. This level of financial inclusion is unprecedented and has the potential to drive economic growth in developing nations.

Another key feature of DeFi is its transparency. Traditional financial systems are often opaque, with hidden fees and complex terms. DeFi platforms, on the other hand, operate on open-source code that is accessible to anyone. This transparency builds trust and reduces the risk of fraud. For global trade, this means that businesses can engage in financial transactions with greater confidence, knowing that the terms of the agreement are clear and enforceable. This section explores how DeFi is being used in trade finance, from supply chain financing to invoice factoring.

However, DeFi is not without its risks. The lack of regulation in the space has led to concerns about security and stability. Hacks and exploits are not uncommon, and the volatility of crypto assets can pose a risk to users. This chapter examines the challenges facing DeFi, from regulatory uncertainty to technological vulnerabilities. It also looks at the efforts being made to address these issues, from the development of more secure smart contracts to the creation of decentralized insurance platforms.

In conclusion, this chapter highlights the transformative potential of DeFi in global trade. By providing accessible, transparent, and efficient financial services, DeFi is democratizing access to capital and enabling new forms of economic activity. However, the space is still in its early stages, and the challenges are significant. As we move forward, the continued development and adoption of DeFi will play a crucial role in redrawing the map of global trade.

5

Chapter 5: The Geopolitical Implications of Crypto

The rise of cryptocurrency is not just a technological or economic phenomenon—it is also a geopolitical one. This chapter explores how crypto is reshaping the global balance of power, challenging the dominance of traditional financial systems and creating new opportunities for nations and individuals alike. From the role of stablecoins in international trade to the use of crypto as a tool for economic sanctions, this section delves into the complex interplay between cryptocurrency and geopolitics.

One of the most significant geopolitical implications of crypto is its potential to undermine the dominance of the US dollar in global trade. For decades, the dollar has been the world's reserve currency, used in the majority of international transactions. Cryptocurrencies, however, offer an alternative. Stablecoins like USDT and USDC, which are pegged to the dollar, are increasingly being used in cross-border trade, providing a more efficient and cost-effective way to transact. This section explores the implications of this shift, from the potential decline of dollar hegemony to the rise of new financial powers.

Another key issue is the use of cryptocurrency as a tool for economic sanctions. Traditional sanctions rely on the control of financial systems, but crypto's decentralized nature makes it difficult to enforce. This has led to concerns about the use of crypto by sanctioned nations and individuals to bypass restrictions. At the same time, crypto has also been used as a tool for resistance, enabling individuals in authoritarian regimes to access financial services and protect their wealth. This chapter examines the dual role of crypto in geopolitics, from its use as a tool of state power to its potential as a force for liberation.

The rise of crypto has also led to a new form of competition among nations. Some countries, like El Salvador, have embraced cryptocurrency, adopting it as legal tender and integrating it into their economies. Others, like China, have taken a more cautious approach, developing their own digital currencies while cracking down on decentralized crypto. This section explores the different strategies being pursued by nations around the world and the implications for global trade. It also looks at the role of international organizations in shaping the future of crypto regulation.

In conclusion, this chapter highlights the profound geopolitical implications of cryptocurrency. By challenging the dominance of traditional financial systems and creating new opportunities for economic activity, crypto is reshaping the global balance of power. However, the space is still in its early stages, and the challenges are significant. As we move forward, the interplay between cryptocurrency and geopolitics will continue to be a defining feature of the global trade landscape.

6

Chapter 6: The Role of Stablecoins in Global Trade

Stablecoins have emerged as a key player in the world of cryptocurrency, offering the stability of fiat currencies with the efficiency of blockchain technology. This chapter explores the role of stablecoins in global trade, from their use in cross-border payments to their potential as a reserve currency. By providing a stable and efficient medium of exchange, stablecoins are bridging the gap between traditional finance and the crypto economy, enabling new forms of trade and economic activity.

One of the most significant advantages of stablecoins is their stability. Unlike volatile cryptocurrencies like Bitcoin, stablecoins are pegged to a stable asset, such as the US dollar or gold. This makes them ideal for use in global trade, where price stability is crucial. For example, a business can use a stablecoin to pay a supplier without worrying about the value of the currency fluctuating before the transaction is completed. This section explores the different types of stablecoins and their use cases in global trade, from remittances to supply chain financing.

Another key feature of stablecoins is their efficiency. Traditional cross-border payments can take days to process and incur high fees. Stablecoins, by contrast, enable near-instant transfers at a fraction of the cost. This has made them particularly popular in the remittance market, where they are being used to send money across borders quickly and cheaply. This chapter examines the impact of stablecoins on the remittance industry, from reducing costs to increasing financial inclusion.

However, stablecoins are not without their challenges. The lack of regulation in the space has led to concerns about transparency and stability. Some stablecoins have been accused of not having sufficient reserves to back their tokens, raising questions about their reliability. This section explores the regulatory landscape for stablecoins, from the efforts of governments to create a framework for their use to the role of decentralized stablecoins in providing an alternative to centralized models.

In conclusion, this chapter highlights the transformative potential of stablecoins in global trade. By providing a stable and efficient medium of exchange, stablecoins are enabling new forms of trade and economic activity. However, the space is still in its early stages, and the challenges are significant. As we move forward, the continued development and adoption of stablecoins will play a crucial role in redrawing the map of global trade.

7

Chapter 7: The Impact of Crypto on Supply Chains

Supply chains are the backbone of global trade, connecting producers, manufacturers, and consumers across the world. This chapter explores how cryptocurrency is transforming supply chains, from increasing transparency to reducing costs. By leveraging blockchain technology, crypto is enabling new forms of supply chain management that are more efficient, secure, and sustainable. This section delves into the key innovations in this space and their implications for global trade.

One of the most significant impacts of crypto on supply chains is increased transparency. Traditional supply chains are often opaque, with limited visibility into the movement of goods and the conditions under which they are produced. Blockchain technology, however, provides a transparent and immutable record of every transaction, from the sourcing of raw materials to the delivery of finished products. This section explores how crypto is being used to create more transparent supply chains, from tracking the origin of products to ensuring ethical labor practices.

Another key advantage of crypto in supply chains is efficiency. Traditional supply chain finance is often slow and cumbersome, with multiple intermediaries adding layers of complexity. Cryptocurrencies, by contrast, enable direct transactions between parties, reducing the need for intermediaries and speeding up the process. This chapter examines the role of crypto in supply chain finance, from invoice factoring to trade credit. It also looks at the use of smart contracts to automate supply chain processes, from payment to delivery.

However, the adoption of crypto in supply chains is not without its challenges. The integration of blockchain technology requires significant investment in infrastructure and training. There are also concerns about the scalability of blockchain networks and the energy consumption of proof-of-work systems. This section explores the challenges facing the adoption of crypto in supply chains, from technological limitations to regulatory uncertainty.

In conclusion, this chapter highlights the transformative potential of crypto in supply chains. By increasing transparency, reducing costs, and improving efficiency, crypto is enabling new forms of supply chain management that are more sustainable and resilient. However, the space is still in its early stages, and the challenges are significant. As we move forward, the continued development and adoption of crypto in supply chains will play a crucial role in redrawing the map of global trade.

8

Chapter 8: The Future of Trade Finance

Trade finance is a critical component of global trade, providing the liquidity and risk management needed to facilitate transactions. This chapter explores how cryptocurrency is transforming trade finance, from reducing costs to increasing accessibility. By leveraging blockchain technology and smart contracts, crypto is enabling new forms of trade finance that are more efficient, transparent, and inclusive. This section delves into the key innovations in this space and their implications for global trade.

One of the most significant impacts of crypto on trade finance is the reduction of costs. Traditional trade finance is often expensive, with banks charging high fees for services like letters of credit and trade loans. Cryptocurrencies, by contrast, enable direct transactions between parties, reducing the need for intermediaries and lowering costs. This section explores how crypto is being used to reduce the cost of trade finance, from peer-to-peer lending to decentralized trade credit.

Another key advantage of crypto in trade finance is accessibility. Traditional trade finance is often inaccessible to small and medium-sized enterprises (SMEs), which lack the collateral and credit history needed to secure financing. Cryptocurrencies, however, provide an alternative by enabling decentralized lending platforms that are open to anyone with an internet connection. This chapter examines the role of crypto in increasing access to trade finance, from supply chain financing to invoice factoring.

However, the adoption of crypto in trade finance is not without its challenges. The lack of regulation in the space has led to concerns about fraud and money laundering. There are also concerns about the volatility of crypto assets and the risk of default. This section explores the challenges facing the adoption of crypto in trade finance, from regulatory uncertainty to technological vulnerabilities.

In conclusion, this chapter highlights the transformative potential of crypto in trade finance. By reducing costs, increasing accessibility, and improving efficiency, crypto is enabling new forms of trade finance that are more inclusive and sustainable. However, the space is still in its early stages, and the challenges are significant. As we move forward, the continued development and adoption of crypto in trade finance will play a crucial role in redrawing the map of global trade.

9

Chapter 9: The Role of Central Bank Digital Currencies (CBDCs)

Central bank digital currencies (CBDCs) are emerging as a key player in the world of cryptocurrency, offering the stability of fiat currencies with the efficiency of blockchain technology. This chapter explores the role of CBDCs in global trade, from their use in cross-border payments to their potential as a reserve currency. By providing a stable and efficient medium of exchange, CBDCs are bridging the gap between traditional finance and the crypto economy, enabling new forms of trade and economic activity.

One of the most significant advantages of CBDCs is their stability. Unlike volatile cryptocurrencies like Bitcoin, CBDCs are issued and backed by central banks, providing the same level of stability as traditional fiat currencies. This makes them ideal for use in global trade, where price stability is crucial. For example, a business can use a CBDC to pay a supplier without worrying about the value of the currency fluctuating before the transaction is completed. This section explores the different types of CBDCs and their use cases in global trade, from remittances to supply chain financing.

Another key feature of CBDCs is their efficiency. Traditional cross-border payments can take days to process and incur high fees. CBDCs, by contrast, enable near-instant transfers at a fraction of the cost. This has made them particularly popular in the remittance market, where they are being used to send money across borders quickly and cheaply. This chapter examines the impact of CBDCs on the remittance industry, from reducing costs to increasing financial inclusion.

However, CBDCs are not without their challenges. The integration of CBDCs into the global financial system requires significant coordination between central banks and international organizations. There are also concerns about privacy and surveillance, as CBDCs could potentially be used to track and monitor transactions. This section explores the challenges facing the adoption of CBDCs, from regulatory uncertainty to technological limitations.

In conclusion, this chapter highlights the transformative potential of CBDCs in global trade. By providing a stable and efficient medium of exchange, CBDCs are enabling new forms of trade and economic activity. However, the space is still in its early stages, and the challenges are significant. As we move forward, the continued development and adoption of CBDCs will play a crucial role in redrawing the map of global trade.

10

Chapter 10: The Environmental Impact of Crypto

The environmental impact of cryptocurrency has become a topic of increasing concern, particularly in the context of global trade. This chapter explores the environmental implications of crypto, from the energy consumption of proof-of-work blockchains to the potential for crypto to drive sustainable practices. By examining both the challenges and opportunities, this section provides a balanced perspective on the role of crypto in creating a more sustainable global trade system.

One of the most significant environmental challenges of crypto is the energy consumption of proof-of-work blockchains like Bitcoin. The process of mining, which involves solving complex mathematical problems to validate transactions, requires vast amounts of energy. This has led to concerns about the carbon footprint of crypto and its impact on climate change. This section explores the environmental impact of proof-of-work blockchains, from the energy consumption of mining operations to the potential for renewable energy to mitigate these effects.

Another key issue is the electronic waste generated by crypto mining. The specialized hardware used in mining, such as ASICs, has a limited lifespan and often ends up as e-waste. This chapter examines the environmental impact of crypto mining hardware, from the extraction of raw materials to the disposal of obsolete equipment. It also looks at the potential for recycling and repurposing mining hardware to reduce e-waste.

However, crypto also has the potential to drive sustainable practices in global trade. Blockchain technology can be used to create more transparent and efficient supply chains, reducing waste and improving resource management. For example, blockchain can be used to track the origin of products, ensuring that they are produced in an environmentally sustainable manner. This section explores the potential for crypto to drive sustainability in global trade, from supply chain transparency to carbon credits.

In conclusion, this chapter highlights the complex environmental impact of crypto. While the energy consumption and e-waste generated by crypto mining are significant challenges, the potential for crypto to drive sustainable practices in global trade is also substantial. As we move forward, the continued development and adoption of crypto will play a crucial role in creating a more sustainable global trade system.

11

Chapter 11: The Role of Regulation in Shaping the Future of Crypto

Regulation is a critical factor in shaping the future of cryptocurrency and its impact on global trade. This chapter explores the role of regulation in the crypto space, from the efforts of governments to create a framework for its use to the challenges of enforcing regulations in a decentralized system. By examining the regulatory landscape, this section provides a comprehensive understanding of the opportunities and challenges facing the adoption of crypto in global trade.

One of the most significant challenges of regulating crypto is its decentralized nature. Unlike traditional financial systems, which are controlled by centralized institutions, crypto operates on a decentralized network that is not subject to the same level of oversight. This has led to concerns about fraud, money laundering, and tax evasion. This section explores the challenges of regulating a decentralized system, from the difficulty of enforcing regulations to the potential for regulatory arbitrage.

Another key issue is the lack of international coordination in crypto regulation. Different countries have taken different approaches to regulating crypto, from outright bans to embracing it as legal tender. This chapter examines the impact of these differing regulatory approaches on global trade, from the fragmentation of the crypto market to the potential for regulatory competition. It also looks at the role of international organizations in creating a coordinated regulatory framework for crypto.

However, regulation also has the potential to drive innovation in the crypto space. By providing a clear legal framework, regulation can increase confidence in crypto and encourage its adoption in global trade. This section explores the potential for regulation to drive innovation, from the development of new financial products to the creation of more secure and efficient blockchain networks.

In conclusion, this chapter highlights the critical role of regulation in shaping the future of crypto and its impact on global trade. While the challenges of regulating a decentralized system are significant, the potential for regulation to drive innovation and increase confidence in crypto is also substantial. As we move forward, the continued development of a coordinated regulatory framework will play a crucial role in redrawing the map of global trade.

12

Chapter 12: The Future of Global Trade in a Crypto-Driven World

As we look to the future, it is clear that cryptocurrency will play a central role in shaping the global trade landscape. This final chapter explores the potential for a crypto-driven world, from the rise of decentralized finance to the integration of blockchain technology into every aspect of trade. By examining the opportunities and challenges ahead, this section provides a vision for the future of global trade in a world where crypto is the norm.

One of the most significant opportunities of a crypto-driven world is the potential for greater financial inclusion. By providing access to financial services for underserved populations, crypto has the potential to drive economic growth and reduce poverty. This section explores the potential for crypto to create a more inclusive global trade system, from enabling small businesses to access global markets to providing financial services for individuals in developing nations.

Another key opportunity is the potential for greater efficiency and transparency in global trade. By leveraging blockchain technology, crypto can create more efficient and transparent supply chains, reducing costs and improving resource management. This chapter examines the potential for crypto to drive efficiency and transparency in global trade, from supply chain management to trade finance.

However, the transition to a crypto-driven world is not without its challenges. The volatility of crypto assets, the lack of regulation, and the environmental impact of crypto mining are all significant hurdles that must be overcome. This section explores the challenges facing the adoption of crypto in global trade, from technological limitations to regulatory uncertainty.

In conclusion, this chapter highlights the transformative potential of crypto in shaping the future of global trade. By providing greater financial inclusion, efficiency, and transparency, crypto has the potential to create a more inclusive and sustainable global trade system. However, the challenges are significant, and the road ahead is uncertain. As we move forward, the continued development and adoption of crypto will play a crucial role in redrawing the map of global trade.

13

Epilogue: The Journey Ahead

The journey of cryptocurrency is just beginning, and its impact on global trade is still unfolding. As we look to the future, it is clear that crypto will continue to play a central role in shaping the global trade landscape. From the rise of decentralized finance to the integration of blockchain technology into every aspect of trade, the potential for crypto to create a more inclusive, efficient, and sustainable global trade system is immense. However, the challenges are significant, and the road ahead is uncertain. As we move forward, the continued development and adoption of crypto will play a crucial role in redrawing the map of global trade. The horizons are unbound, and the future is ours to shape.

Book Description: Horizons Unbound: How Crypto is Redrawing the Map of Global Trade

In *Horizons Unbound: How Crypto is Redrawing the Map of Global Trade*, we embark on a journey into the transformative world of cryptocurrency and its profound impact on global commerce. This book is not just about Bitcoin or blockchain—it's about how these technologies are reshaping the way we exchange value, conduct business, and connect across borders. From the origins of decentralized finance to the rise of stablecoins, decentralized finance (DeFi), and central bank digital currencies (CBDCs), this book explores how crypto is dismantling traditional systems and creating new opportunities for individuals, businesses, and nations alike.

Through 12 insightful chapters, *Horizons Unbound* delves into the technological, economic, and geopolitical shifts driven by cryptocurrency. It examines how crypto is eliminating intermediaries, reducing costs, and increasing efficiency in global trade. It highlights the potential for greater financial inclusion, particularly in developing nations, where access to traditional banking has long been a barrier to economic growth. The book also addresses the challenges—volatility, regulatory uncertainty, environmental concerns—and offers a balanced perspective on the road ahead.

With a focus on real-world applications, the book explores how crypto is revolutionizing supply chains, trade finance, and cross-border payments. It examines the role of stablecoins in facilitating seamless transactions, the potential of DeFi to democratize access to capital, and the geopolitical implications of a crypto-driven world. From the rise of CBDCs to the environmental debate surrounding crypto mining, *Horizons Unbound* provides a comprehensive look at the opportunities and challenges of this new era.

Written in an engaging and accessible style, this book is for anyone curious about the future of global trade. Whether you're a business leader, a policymaker, or simply someone interested in the intersection of technology and economics, *Horizons Unbound* offers a thought-provoking exploration of how cryptocurrency is redrawing the map of global trade—and what it means for the future of our interconnected world.

The horizons are unbound, and the possibilities are endless. This is the story of how crypto is changing the world, one transaction at a time.

www.ingramcontent.com/pod-product-compliance
Lightning Source LLC
LaVergne TN
LVHW020742090526
838202LV00057BA/6179